Threading Stone

by Carey Scott Wilkerson

For my Mother and Father

Library of Congress Control Number: 2017936226
ISBN Number: 978-0-9986857-1-7

Wilkerson, Carey Scott
Threading Stone, poems by Carey Scott Wilkerson

Let me humbly thank the editors and staff of the following publications in which many of these poems, often in a different form, first appeared: Amaryllis, Arden, Atlanta Press, Eratio, Genesee WordLab, Nonce Editions, TheArtsPneumonia, Word for/Word, X-stream, and zafusy. Thanks also to the Lillian E. Smith Center for Creative Arts for a transformative 2009 Writing Fellowship and to Philip Kaplan and Iris Saltiel. I thank and celebrate my friends and colleagues in Columbus State University's Department of English. And, of course, I am grateful to a true genius artist, John Summerfield, and the heroic enterprise New Plains Press.

Published by Summerfield Publishing, New Plains Press, PO Box 1946, Auburn, AL, 36831-1946, using Scribus Open Source Software with Trebuchet MS font. Adobe Stock photo used in cover is *3D Labyrinth or Maze*, by Peter Jurik.

Tablet of Contents

III.

I.

Research and Development

You would not write this
as I would not imagine
these lines in crippled geometries
scaled up for another of your
comprehensive reviews.
True, there remains in all
this a civil resolution though
perhaps one without absolute values,
that magnetic north of deepest learning,
a plunder of concentric betrayals and
ludic impostures.

I need some new material
and some say, perhaps, a ghost lyricist,
unspooling ideas secretly among the marginalia of
your recipes and daybooks, folding himself
into a repertory of nocturnal maneuvers, and, it's true:
looking good from a distance.

As for my own incidental involvement here,
I could say only that objects are suspended
before the gravity of your aesthetic as water before the
solemnity and censure of stone.

(I imagined here immodest claims
about the river in our history, the turn of
forgotten grace in the last instant before
a boat drifts too far from the shore,
spinning, as we all must, on chance
operations flooding through
our sacraments of logic.)

It is a failed program and a failed poem,
which, for now, we will keep to ourselves.

Equivocal Topology

We found the news of this poem alarming
and we trust you will not press us for further comment
as one might document the margins of grace
peeling ghosts from the mirror of your similitudes
I have seen you in the dimming light
folding toward some forgotten form
lost on the plasmic vistas of democracy,
recitations of names in slow erasure
known quantities sluicing away

We remain resolutely opposed to these grammatological songs,
these ruinous texts and endless declensions of alterity.
We want to understand this in terms of simpler conjectures.
There is evidence of a deception here.
in a deepening logic of parody
an end, after all, to ironic shapes
a closure of expressive shadow
a waking from a life in the delirium of scansion
and the cruel freedoms peculiar to the motif of sleep.
I will not have written this.

Late View of a Mill Ruin

You will be surprised to learn
that I went back.
I would like to say it was in the hope
of seeing parts of us there, collected
among the turbine viscera and shredded cable
footnotes of some vague fantasia on parts and wholes.

But in the dim, iron light of a slow
and imprecise memory, I found only
a material density folded into the trace,
opaque and irreducible, to be sure,
a mechanics of hard enterprise and, for me,
an uncertain similitude of what is fixed and what is broken.

Stone's Throw

I need these rocks as they are
not as need is known or
none will lift this common heavy
dimpled monstration wrought on every
imagined gift or playful as a pageant is
a rift between granite desires.

This is how we were taught
to crumble around curves of inquiry
or stumble through monologues, across
cracks in familiar places proved igneous or
given to subduction

The lesson here is strict as sand in your mouth,
pure archaeologies of the tongue and its
proper phantoms, strands of spittle
glistening across the glossary for
the sheer heft of my polished baubles:
Dense and ironic if you please
and rolling just now into traffic.

Oubliette

Here is the escape artist, writhing inside his box
searching for a trapdoor hinged to a seam of light.
He claims to have read somewhere that magic, properly executed
turns the whole world on some secret axis of intensionality.
The truth is he counts to ten and breathes in the hope of darkness,
of dead entanglements and parodies of God.
Finding this untenable, he declares the trick complete
and relocates permanently to the box, removes to the space within.
Reading is, of course, impossible, and he resolves never to explain
a life affixed to right angles shredded under asymptotes and knees.
The audience dies of boredom and the assistant dies of despair.
His visitors are radical skeptics who roll around in spheres.
The church has no official position on the matter;
the academy is divided into the cautious and the querulous.
Memory migrates to those old-time vertices
of scattered voices and physical laws squared away.
But there are limits, he supposes, to what illusions permit
and at last he can claim to have nothing up a sleeve.
It's true enough, however, that he sometimes imagines springing
    suddenly up,
dancing that macabre jig just to prove that it can still be done.

Pronunciation Guide

Say these words as though you
cannot forget the tongue, hidden,
an embarrassment, or a dream
of first principles.

Speak with your hand over
a mouth; there is no certain way
to know if that mouth will be
yours forever, so

Scream under the explicit face
mostly, I think, to test and to taste
the acoustic properties of familiar
settings; this will alarm your friends.

Sing a theoretical tune that
assumes all these words and
goes like a hymn or a dirge or
an anthem or an air.

Urban Ritual

I am trying not to forget the feeling
of that clumsy pirouette I affected
once on West Sixteenth Street.

Well, of course, this was New York,
so nothing else would make sense,
hence, my grammar of dance.

And that was a chance operation,
a kind of ironic meditation on the love
of limits, or caution, or, perhaps,

what is left of beauty when I begin
to count the number of steps from
subway platform to digital sky , or

ask to what degree or, even, why
the real seems to drift, soft-shoe,
across the imagined these days.

It is a perfect world in which
I confess, as much to myself as to anyone,
that I never finally understood ballet.

Modal Triptych

I
 Still Life with Semicolon;

 If the visionary's aesthetic can be
(we are using a term) inferred from
the quantity of else or mad, then
is a suffix, a question of repetition.
This, of course, refers to a time when
an objet d'artifice(?) was presumed to be
where it is, that is, where in fact are held
the twin charms of proof or nothing requiring
a sustained encounter and some old-style
hurt qua thing in a box, better thus.

II
First Study:

makes a plural
envisions perhaps no more than, say, two
as one could not deliver on the promise
or if a third is tracing a known harmonic
acting on a received view, collapsing on a principle
how faster discredits this quantum, a known
interval, placed behind the fragmentary art of:
parlor drollery, effete transgressivism, delusional triumphalism,
a sex polemic or incomplete motion
provisional, perhaps no more

(notes),

And it was said to be a thing extended in [space]
an asymmetrical critique of rules governing implacement.

A lie is that object projected infinitely into logological [continuity]
its vastness a breviary of presumptions, codified in bad faith.

A poet could be imagined as a node of solemnity in doggerel
[milieux]
or as merely taking up, making up the cosmos as a damage report.

This, incidentally, was merely suggestive of a magic duplicity, later
reconsidered as the fundamental duple condition of magic things, a
perception all the more fascinating for its cavalier endorsement of
"the magical" and concomitant rejection of reliable, if
problematical unities.

None of this settles those problems of spatial representation
insofar as it seems to preclude the very terms of its own analysis,
is a terrible disappointment to lovers and to friends

Thus are the dispensations accorded to boundary clowns forever
fused to the axioms of (T)ruth.
There remains some room for work in the taxonomy of syllogisms.

apple epi(stem)ologies are not correctives
to orange mysticisms, or, as some have observed,
a distraction from the dread implications of
stochastic noise reconfigured as structured
thinking - distinguished here from
"thought"

the very thought/the mere thought of it
a cave/a concavity: sophisticates will call this w(hole) procedure
   into question

[13]

III

Detail from First Study:

out of the question:

He does not dare to reveal the contents of the journal
documenting all the places they conjugated that Spring.
All things considered, the "stair" entries are notable
for their coy deployment of the subjunctive tense.

(notes),

proves from the apple a mode of orange
or posits a deep demotic of geometric relations
nowhere charted out to
a vector, a crisis
a someplace dreams through a toy head
And this was thought to be the substrate proper for a discussion
of the vagaries governing blank paper, a white chaos doubling
as the consensual corpse of fashion feeding into metaphysics.
Similarly, your portmanteau notion of the given world as an exit
strategy from the police state of erasure feels like a respectable
madness.
It is, however, only right to confess that in the absence of "the missing
passage," an industry of speculative moves toward the passage seems
entirely satisfying, even authoritative.

Or, to put it another way

[14]

Two Meditations on The Tempest

Sycorax Apologia

Or you could have learned Latin.
Certainly, simple dreamers were happy enough
to remain uncomprehending, remote, diffracted through
your forest idylls and faux barbarisms.
Some thinkers cast Caliban as the bucolic skeptic
reduced by a mother's schemes to rage and madness.
Others believe only in you, mistress of ignominy, shadow,
and prolix visionary of the shimmering latitudes conjured in restless
sleep.
That was how you split the oracular tongue
And how we were admonished and humiliated and reminded
that silence is a healing art.

Ariel's Failed Petition to Prospero

As from your certain proof escapes
The dreamed refuge of a fugitive art,
So, too, your summary truth that drapes,
In dread, the grateful, penitent heart
Will reel and twirl in twilit texts,
Taken to be the pure iteration
Of peeling whorls your whirl inflects,
To knit implicit your purling duration
On quilted skeins of second nature,
Built first on games of nomenclature
Awakened, thus, to nominal eyes, as would be inversely shown,
I take this line my predicate prize, imprisoned by trust,
recursively flown.

Olson In Montevallo

I like to think it happens almost without
anyone noticing: the late approach of his giant shadow,
curling away from the auguries of autumn light
and toward the doubling torque of his chin,
in hortative bounce.
He has come to write a poem of immensity
and of the grace so hard to find in a world
one observes pressing to the margins
of a page, like footnotes swept up in roiling
convections of country perplexity
or bowling balls guttered in architectonic rhapsodies.

The clay down here spackles his trousers,
a drop-cloth lost to the larger world but proof
that we, too, know how to treat our abstract expressionists.
Indeed, it is to the north that our best poets dream, but then again
everything--even Jacksonville, Florida--is north of Alabama.
Don't worry about whether his projective Earth wobbles on an axis
between Montevallo and Gloucester or whether one can discern,
from the words alone, his view of death and its discontents.
It is enough to know that even vast, voluble Okeanos himself
drinks from the Chattahoochee when the water is cold.

St. Augustine's Algorithm

"What have I to say to you,
beyond the usual congratulatory gestures?" my first question might
have been.

I expect you can sense the confession concealed here.
Still, none but the most churlish - and you are not among them -
would dismiss these moments as platitudes, as failed appeals for
blessings on the vague substrate of veiled beatitudes. This is what I
have become.

You know perfectly well that even rogue sinners like me
can summon some semblance of light in sleight of hand and winter
reverie.

I, too, have a mother and have been surprised by visions of death
and have wondered, even as I imagined my own, whether my living
love will be responsive to a woman's secret heart, whether in fact
the deepening dark of the year is not a harbinger of some dying
vine in those gardens of faith, an abstraction that flourishes in your
admonitions.

Still, you must know, before you go, that whatever else is true of me
is true from the first formulation to the last polyplicative
instantiation.

I am, in equal proportions, a man and a clown.
But I believe in beauty when it proves through its transient humility
that if my eyes are finally open, my head is your image in stone.

[17]

Fabulae Praetextae:

[...] thus, a return to the very
tradition it presumed to replace.

Use only the good parts from the
Epilogue to fill in the details we need
for the Prologue, which in this case is
an encomium styled as Monologue. Or:

did we mean to say an encominum-style Monologue
*rethink either 1) the minscule "e" in encomium (clumsy phrase)
or 2) the majuscules in: Epi-, Pro-, and well, you know
what I mean.

this arch academic harmonic in everything we compose is
becoming more a recourse than a resource, which is
another thing: about this question of documentation,
all it seems to me that required is not, what, the authority, but
rather the authenticity of the past (well, the prior, not to put too
fine a point on it):
history, contiunity, synthesis, and all that

it's where we come from, how we began,
the origo fontium of our imputed heritage.

(thats a nice line, we can use that elsewhere,
which reminds me, we cannot use highfalutin Latin words
in the title AND in the body of this work)

*but, as I said that origo fontium moment is compelling,
so it must go, and I'll use it
later,
again,
for the first time

II.

Rural Routes

You said you wish I were more communicative,
so I am telling you now that I have
complicated feelings about kudzu.
Observe its vines seducing our telephone wires,
its filaments tickling through my conspiracy of
whispered conceits.
I could say I am growing eager just to test the spatial
properties of my deceptions, the way one just supplants another
with a certain seed of aplomb,
but I want to be honest about my kudzu,
its misappropriation of the given world arcing
away from our hands and dirt in a semiotics of entanglement.

I have always understood my kudzu was never the pliant rotation,
of domestic vegetable you had wanted but, rather,
a dream of looping tendrils and indecorous curlings
through the rhizomic root-ball of desire, love's wet roots,
reaching out of themselves, a rhetoric of cords and splines.
You won't have to tell the neighbors why I moved to the
back yard, into my mother's, two-tone green Chevelle,
a topiary now, absurd on blocks, my inquiry into
savage florologies on certain rural routes,
rust and rind in my kiss.

Give us, then, this kudzu, our native tongue in bitter pulp,
peeling paper of leaves and palimpsests in the Alabama mud.
Give us kudzu twine in Ariadne's clue, reasoning backward
to the terminus in summer's skein, threading through August mists,
Minotauric arts of return, secret recursions across dirt-road republics

[23]

held by reduplicative snare in the unwinding yarn
of my poem's splitting pods and redolent blooms,
a truth of kudzu in the binding of my books, the light across my
   table,
the patterns on your sundress, the philosophy of my harvest,
the intorsions of our sleep.

Rape of the Book

Whom do we find here but our man in the poem
Felix Omega himself, a known purveyor
of fraudulent philosophy, and
thinking today of stealing, from the library, a derelict
edition of Spinoza's Ethics.
His fingers map the opened gutter between pages splayed
before his immodest gaze, the heat of his palm pressing the spine
upward to his nose, eyelashes dusting the atoms
from a first edition's fine mill, an untouched text's uncertain
surrender.
Axioms bend and quiver in stylized inversions,
claims sliding in panels of dark relation toward disjunctive aporia,
a fold of corollary under a crease of sweet scholia.
the circulation card ripped in a contrapositive shudder.
Love, he supposes, must move in this way, through tears
and cuts in some exigent whiteness, seduction inscribed as
a maquillage of knowledge on the space of submission,
empty sets in the concentric circles of desire,
the memory of its final lines, its last passage
into closure, a rebuke to the violence of deep learning.
But here is no dream of a readerly deliverance from the ignominy
of phantoms among the stacks.
This book is his now.
It belongs to him.

Rock-Quarry Wall Graffiti for Felix

There has been talk of an emerging periodicity,
precisely the kind of speculative prattle that
compels us to imagine stylized departures,
wave cycles of constitutive games.

Of course, this thesis turns entirely
on the twin axes of lost referents
and certain grim proprieties of faith.
We have wondered to what degree this
represents your characteristic motion,
the (igne)ous differential in tracing against
your own quilted scrims of memory.

And then there was the fear that
we could not bear the necessary incompleteness
or survive its noumenal marbling of desire.
What, then, to make of this fugitive talking,
codes of displacement negotiated at the frontier's
edge, the disappearing evidence?

Yours is that machine of an else in madness,
recombinant touch and go, nomenclatures in parallax,
unconfirmed rumors of a message received

Felix, Styx, and Stone

We are speaking here of that moment when
Felix Omega, you know the one, declares
that it was all an equivocation, a kind of epistemological
antic and that, properly understood, these gestures
cannot be properly understood.
But we hasten to point out that ghosts inside your name does not
impute credibility to these misadventures: now an outrageous
assertion, now a crippling paranoia ...
Indeed, who among us will not agree that ritual modes exchanged,
transmuted in the lambent light of machine's deep becomes the
closure of clown's logic. There is surely no point in denying a certain
ambivalence attendant upon the procedures; yet if the effect is
negligible, the affect is most singular, not to say, silly:
Lucent else runs in snaking brocade through composite glyphs and
frames of fog.

As a rule, we hold restrict our notes to asynchronous rejoinders
and asymptotic marginalia. Here then, if you believe the reports, is
Felix, penitent narcissist, affable bumbler, a good man withal.
Pretending to be the scion of country mystics or a foundling,
transposed during odd eruptions of weather, he is, in some sense, the
flâneur manqué, alive in the city we forgot, a generative principle
derived from objects between his own epiphanies.
You are love in footnotes, Felix, or it is your notation we want
as we have learned to believe in the style of provocation, paper to
seeming, slow to illusion, a hermetic drift in the given world.

Which is how we know a hand or curling reach
is left to take from a place or polity the numbers
of making as none or flown or truncate, a sliver is
you read as a facing does remain a theory,
a structure; and, to be sure, a programmatic thrust
or moving thus toward some end point
arcs of charge and yes those convictions
were said to be deeply felt or held or in any case

You will know how to read it
as from the first reflex to build is
certain places on rubrics, a further, a letter.
Then and purely a matter of last, it seems clear
if such is keep or can be seen as sequence
parts of larger and pressed to legible perceptions
particle theory of speechification or maybe the wave
You will know how to read it
plural integration to thread and still this
retrieve where mapping from what a face is

Writing to the Horizon

The page is flat, as no Earth ever was,
even as its own world must be. And you
are here, as none other can presume
to know what is provable, what is round,
as theories of infinite return, the looping
chorus of memory, the trust one places
in one place or another.

To be at all, things have to be where they are,
as paper is, as sooner or later is written over the line
breaking with its past, ambivalent about
the state of play at the margins, at the center,
at the expense of a circumscribed life or
at the risk of seeming not to believe
in the face of a lover.

A map is unrolled, as some flags have been
known to argue the facts of folding, furling
for what is coherent, if any is left to discern
the results of experiments at the frontier,
of adventures in bad penmanship
concealing scribbles and doodles,
in the trace, to discover.

Felix Finds a Folio

Looking back, it was bound to fail these tests,
these improvisations. And who among us would be
fool enough to write down the names of those involved?
Maybe "puzzling" was not, in the end, quite the right word for
what it became:

give us, then, our minimal fictive transgressions, as it is our
this, too, is within the expected, acceptable(?) and ritually a
forge topographically only remote in the guise of rules toward
or precipitate and causatively transplode such if need keep ply:
else complot from or quince is a known hyacinth, a trust he
and lyrical, some referent as drifting down, as the plume
replete with but for none among beyond who speaks is this
how reticulate, thrall other tensile over of transitive to tessurae:
sum knot if a plex is return or intrinsicate my peeling variable
framing your and gone proved simpler, not vague
rather, too, or fabulations with some do work

Felix forgets to read the codes and is lost
to his found objects of grace. Or, he is consigned
to some wistful vision of the trobar clus
inscribed between the mediating planes of his happy life.
He will speak to this question in a conversation
with a woman he has never met:

He: I am thinking about how it happens that one can cling to
clearly unsupported assertions.
She: Do I know you?

[30]

He: Well, that's just it you see.
She: I don't follow.
He: Which is why I know you'll understand how I have gotten by so
long on this shaky premise.

Felix is not a reliable correspondent,
and the mail is often a speculative project,
something joyfully conceived between
parenthetical identities.

Years earlier, he had imagined himself
composing these same phantom lines
and sending them into perplexity's
library of doggerel and dross. Only
in this scenario, there is another
solitary reader who happens on the
derelict lines and finds, in them,
the sound of a voice of his own.

Theseus to Ariadne

Prayer is the native tongue of lost men.
And I have, it seems, only my words to blame
for this errant fantasy, this absurd tableau:
kissing you on the Labyrinth steps, my
bumbling, over-rehearsed soliloquy,
something about righteous gestures of vengeance.

Incidentally, it was kind of you to give me this yarn,
privately, I supposed, to spare my vanity.
I have a certain vision of its symbolic importance
unspooling across history and art, although
I'm not so sure about love.
In any case, I am struck just now by how much of
what is received as triumphal and good is built
on conspiracy and double dealing.

As Ovid will tell it, the Minotaur itself, himself(?) is two-formed,
is a formulation of doubleness, a formal duplicity!
Of course, I would not dare to suggest that this perhaps maps
the hero and the monstrosity onto the same coordinates, no
indeed not.

I'm only saying that it compels
me to wonder about the language of the Minotaur's own prayers
and wonder whether he, too, feels imprisoned
in an identity not strictly his own,
and if at our meeting
it is possible for us to see in each
other something of ourselves.

[32]

The Felix Predicates: A Polylogue in Four Parts

Dear Grammo,

I am writing to you somewhat in the manner of the Felix appearing
in section two of the document appended below.

(Listen, don't trust him; there is no Felix;
 Yes, there have been certain other "correspondents,"
[quotes added later]

 but this F__x is a fraudulent representation)

I leave to you the matter of whether any of this constitutes poetry.

(because, of course, he imagines himself the laureate manqué
 of a collapsed tradition of versification without justification and,
moreover, did we forget to say, don't trust him(!)?)

or prose, or, indeed, some fugitive form.*

(*for which we wouldn't give nine cents to save the last dime in
Christendom; to say nothing of how this whole "Dear Grammo"
gambit is too droll by half)

Respectfully,

(Insert nom de plume here)

[33]

Partition One

which is to say, rolling disclosure, a mapping if summary
connectives review thus an exigent, a fixity, not probabalistic
intensional paper plan or number theory for refinements in
hagiographic clusters, whereupon a parallel duplicity may be
discerned, but by whom a cleansing formulation in draft, in (ek)
or state funded striganomical, umbraical projects are or are far
from, so far as we know, a properly interdisciplinary sample
graphic trend dynamic correlation or façon de parler so to speak

Notes Toward a Felix

I. As Theoretician With Tools For Solitary Work

From his study, good Minos may have seen
the consequences for members of the convocation,
trundling our hero in some stylized conveyance
to the columnar plinths of the labyrinth gate.
Indeed, one might conclude that in this mise en scéne,
there exists the one true value-free zone of inquiry,
the ontology of the hidden.
This is to inquire whether it remains an accepted axiom that
good things are knowable by the style of their derelictions.
For my own records, I note that it is possible
to think of these relations in terms of our querulous
career petitioners to truth, the same ones
who prattle endlessly on about the discourse of ruin, in the discourse
of ruin.

I cannot pretend to have arrived at any clarity on this
matter, but I confess that merely invoking the problem
gives me some sense of entitlement, a kind of proprietary
claim to its more controversial formulations.
And, incidentally, because so much of this seems wholly
indefensible, I am declaring it an economy of scale and -
therefore - idiomatically, nothing but my own, indeed, truly,
mine.

[35]

Partition Two

that said, a current or true currency of interpolation self-
contained non-restrictive mechanics becomes the evolving
standardized ineluctable derivation as of the closing bell curving
upward against predicted supply chain letters of resignation,
commendation, and (ek) an indeterminate outward discarded
from the file; in common parlance we do not say "in common
parlance," but restore coordination among select branches in
remaining trees thought to lie beyond accepted frontier, solvency
to an nth speculative, velocity to the symmetrical politesse

Judicious Excisions:

none but this, then, for a harlequin's despair,
his habitation of games, votive perplexity
for auxiliary saints and their coteries of
revenants in the card catalog

(We were measuring the twilight for
stars, draped in the monastic threads
of winter's memory, our shadows, a liturgy in
ambiguous flourishes, the broken signature
of a day ending itself for the greater, you know, good.)

**there seems also to have been a dispute
over pronouns with Felix as an antecedent

** him, it, and they?

[37]

Partition Three

equanimity to the real as when we permit enough trope to hang a
self with in the public square of opposition revised according to
footnotes appended to the codicil on the just application of the
classical model in which are presumed to be held lessons for
each, all, every, any and as the line approaches the Y axis, so,
too, does the quantity converge infinitely close to the zero sum
game play with approved representations of implicit transactions
among the good people of the (ek)static intorsions intrinsications
per capita dissembling magnifica not to say a coterie of charmers
with rhymes pinned to designer eschatologies in the manner of
your gourmand cannibal critics with credit and credentials
enough to consume entire archaeologies of thought in time it
takes to produce a declaration of consensus

II. A Bon Vivant Of The Decorous Quasi Compilatam***

Good Sir,

Before we get to the important news regarding the matter you raised in your last (enclosed), I want to amuse you with some doggerel from this week's plunder, remarks by an anonymous writer of eleventh century Lobbes--now Belgium--on whether one can discern, from a written text alone, the authenticity of saintly miracles:

"As the innumerable and manifest merits of these fathers combined surpass the eloquence of all the wise rhetors, lest someone whisper that, nevertheless, we have coined a fabulous lie, the pen of this story (which has been undertaken) proclaims unequivocally not the dreamy records of some sort of falsification, but the past works of an amazing virtue" (?)

I take this to mean that the improbable is somehow self-authorizing or, indeed, that the unbelievable is credible evidence for its own truth. Now, there are obviously some larger issues to be addressed before I can sell that on the street, but the logic here is so provocative and asymmetric, I have taken it up as a kind of template for good living. Of course, you can see that this relates, however obliquely, to the substance of my project. Moreover, as I have made real progress since last we spoke, it is no small pleasure to discover now a legitimate historical program for my motivations, which are yet unclear even to me. But I have no reservations about my choice of material.

[39]

*

** everybody's doing it

Incidentally, I don't know that Whitman ever declared Leaves of Grass an epic, but I can report that it sure copies like one, to say nothing of the odd delight one finds in reproducing the pagination in every detail. Naturally, I am using the 1892 "Deathbed" edition which was itself an expansion, a revisited revision, and, therefore, a copy. And although I wonder what moral implications it might have for the final draft, surely turning back now would be more perverse than having begun at all, not least because every word is so extraordinarily good. Indeed, I feel as though they are my own and I am evr yr hmbl svnt,

F___x

[40]

Partition Four

in accordance with a crystalization of implementations formerly
ratified but only now taking effect and cause right along with
them to the floor for further polyplication and particle oversight
up to and including but not limited to such enumerated
constraints as could be seen to proscribe a prescriptivist
inscription, that is: arrivals and departures (ek) by which is
understood a conic section subtending our working schematics
for the new home of the Halawaukee Institute for Exegetical
Arts, a buried lead

Enclosure:

(Felix, if that is your name, I know what you're up to. And if it is true that I confess a secret fascination with the project, then it is also true that you deserve my candor. To that end, I am in the unenviable position of having to warn you that some things are more permissible than others and some things, not at all!

querulously,

....) Grammo Pro(xy), esq, implicit as an egg

Partition Five

matter of fact, now that you mention it, if we might, high
expectations duly lowered, at least to the median level of water
passing through the Bean Mill tributary, a local issue really, little
appreciated in other parts of the (ek) of the Free; plasticity then
is a question for outcome measures

III. The Penitent Phenomenologist

My confession will not precipitate
the kind of shock that follows
a storm's opening paragraph.
Taken together, my many claims are perhaps too
modest and do not constitute the revelation
you deserve, the disclosure you demand.
I could propagate through a doomed medium
of secret glyphs, as fear pressing some forgotten
November sky down into our silent food, into
our glib assertions, our calendars of deception.
I could further conceal all this with ritual vanities
in the guise of heroism, art, my entire repertory of
comic tempests and charitable distractions.
But you, because you have waited with me for
the inversions of history to right themselves,
cannot now pretend I was never standing on my head.

Strangely, having admitted this much, I wonder whether
it is fair for me to declare absolution because we both know,
don't we, that what I am about to say will not survive
even in the gentle light that shows us how to die
in so many words,
Grammo,
Compilo,
Daddy-O.

[44]

Partition Six

and the tyranny of Delta T, the journal of portents, a reliquary
of dread composites, a grimoire of sinister chortles and middle
managers, men with many keys, women with intersticial
methdologies imputed downward through the viscera, this
doomed body of electric else; false alarums, false allegations;
move along; nothing to see here.

IV. Cartographic Elegy On The Occasion
Of Felix's Late Arrival

Because we made maps together,
I can see properly through the
unmeasured intervals of our loss, plot a trajectory of
my missed opportunities, or, as the legend has it,
an emerging lifetime of miscues, Grammo's notes make no
reference to this part:
It is not perversity, but in fact a hard honesty that
compels me to insist upon some aesthetic recovery of
my failure, a modicum of ruin held between us,
of the systems that fell beneath our
crushing hysteria for spelling out, by turns, our
humility, our platitudes, even our secret disdain
in the damaged topography of freedom.

We are the last patriots in a vanishing republic of shame.

Of course, we could cry over these spilled coordinates;
or we could claim it was all a question of scale.
The truth is I never believed in your autonomy and
certainly never wanted it for myself. These borders are
indeterminate, indefensible and transgression, too simple.
It would be love spoken in sophistic tones to remind you
that the boundary of demarcation separating each of us
from the other and both of us from some uncharted region
is a necessary condition of all three. But keep that to yourself.
I confess it is not heroic, but the dismissal of grim warnings on
the frontier of a betrayal is a lesson I would teach all innocence,
a dark curriculum of fatalism and diffidence that leaves me
wandering ever away from you in wider and stranger circles,
finding nonetheless, that

[46]

it all looks so familiar, as though you
had been here
before.
The usual questions of timing
were at issue, and I think also
the problem of propriety.

It was a Saturday spent transposing
one quantity of betrayal into the corresponding harmonic
of resignation. Or it was the ghastly spectacle of two
lovers imprecisely affixing dark humor
to a variation on the same ironic failure
of putative Mouths, or:

I am some dissident Felix.

Let's call it a theory of imbrications
even open books are not finally "open" in the sense
that logos requires - let's say desires - some old-fashioned topoi,
enough space to work, to dig down through the record, to
operate on the principle of closure, but quietly, in the guise of
plain
memory dissolving with yet more modulations
of our daily business, let's call it "us."
So, speaking to all this is a matter of some urgency and has a
texture, as confession, as revelation, as sudden clarity, let's call
it "the self-referential."
If it will make you more comfortable, I can go first, just simply
start, or let's call it "begin" with some
halcyon and pastoral observations:
And to your left, a eucalyptus tree,
or in any case, our speculative approach
to the "eucalyptus" idiom, an informed précis,
actually, of some related thematic material:

[48]

Off to the right - and this is an
unscripted appearance! - the Problem
of Spatial Relations, known in the quaint
bucolic vernacular as anything that can be done to a logarithm;
but how will our grammarians come to terms with
the received view that you can take the boy (ek) out
of the city, but not the city, etc: rain forests, soil erosion,
magnolia qua marginalia, Horace's Eclogues, on and on.
Now, of course, we return to the glistening rhizomes
of the midtown interchange, the chromium ventricles of
our reflexive concentricities, Grammo on the colonnade,
a primordial monstration of glyphs in the perpendicular:
reinforced concrete,
a vertical, flâneur epistemology,
the names of a closing sky,
our second nature, and,
if you can believe it,
the imperiled Ozone, melting polar cap,
bumble bee extinction, what have you.

the lost, last Felix of our
possible world.

Notes Toward a Failed Theory

Thank you for this sonnet, which I regard
as evidence of the good will between us
and more than merely suggestive of
the strangeness developing around here.
I used to believe the logical positivists were converging
onto something determinate, a real insight
into the structure of the given world;
now, I'm not so sure. This is why
I am mixing milk with my algebra and
faith with formalism; but the truth, if any remains,
is off the record, a mélange of texture and gesture,
a syncopated wiggle of providential fat.

P.S. The view from the couplet is good
        and gathers us toward its faltering light.

[50]

III.

for the City of Los Angeles

Labyrinth Studies

I

Here, I suppose, are the clarities I had hoped
would be my evidence against
accretions of bad templates:
the simple opposed to the complex
the virtuous opposed to the merely amused
the puzzled contented opposed to, say,
                    the tragic-comically quizzical.

This argument—if it is one—is incomplete
without the dutiful recourse to my habituation
(let's call it a "sense of propriety")
for impaling the whole
upon the shards of the parts.

Viewed from above, this is the traditional
reflexive move toward self-inquiry
and happy classical liberalism.

From below, it is, perhaps a repudiation
of the premises in something like:

"Rules are for bankers and botanists"

or:

"The cat may give birth to her kittens in the oven,
but that doesn't make them biscuits."

This is how I live.

Increasingly, however, the view is parallax
to the usual distortions
and is both more and less compelling
than the prevailing vogue
for educated second-guessing
would lead us to believe.

But I have standards,
and to find the most
convincing cosmology in your tortured
footnotes would hardly be surprising,
would be no surprise at all.

2

Look straight ahead, Theseus.
This will have been you or one of your unresolved knots
bound in philosophical commitments, dreaming in the dark
and tracing, as from particles stretched on the plane of your
corners a skein of shadow draping from seams pressed in the
   putative walls

Look, Thesues, into your rhizomic world.
Think of all that will have revealed itself in ruptures of radical
concealment affixed to speculative vanishing points, end times,
   game theories
Think of the partitions in your name: These Us
and eschatologies of deep disclosure and indeterminate modes
   of address

Thesues, look at what you have done.
Know that if you will have been a hero, then some too will have
         forgotten you, pleased indeed to have
         imagined you
         irretrievably ensnared in some vague narrative line
         about finding oneself.

You will not have been conjecture or song or existential place-
   holder
something aporetic in the causal chain, plural synthesis of
   apriori singulars
These are your monsters, real or imagined, and you cannot know
what they mean to us who will have known you to wander, as
from terminus to tangle, threading the stone through
recombinant night.

[55]

3

We will take this to be a door
aperture of faith, of absolute values

opening to the drift of apprehensions
in programs discerned from the inside out

closing, surely, to the entreaties to the authorities
to the rubbings you made of guarded graves

We observe its gentle arc and are implicated
in its implicit mapping of

a territorial expropriation, a boundary condition
and this we take to be our missionary aesthetic,

one of crossing over and moving through
and entrance into entranced spaces.

4

of the shape or else a shaping tool
a referent

I bend into an America that is other
than the polity or a pronouncement
and yet am impelled toward some
nomological structure, a trust in
that which derives from

the late convictions of the fool
for his antecedents

deep thinkers correctly rebuke me
for failing to carve out a position
but this rock looks right to me
and I feel it would be immoral
to interfere with what, for all I know,
is a work already,
if imperceptibly,
in progress,
as work might be seen in
my maze of raw materials,
cracking perhaps a pattern of love
through miracula merita multimoda,
through fabula when the fracture appears

[57]

5

St. Thomas never proclaimed himself either an existentialist or a realist—though for that matter he never said he was a Thomist.
                                                                    -- Jacques Maritain

I yam what I yam.
          -- Popeye

Minotaur, your head, your horns
are those of a bull,
and it seems to me
that I cannot count
on your having a sense
of humor about it.

So here is what I am proposing:
a symposium on
the Problem of the Minotaur,
a Mintotauria Prolematica.

It is saying almost nothing to suggest
that maybe the real issue here
is not so much one of disambiguation,
that is, differentiation, as, rather,
simply rethinking the name.

I certainly would not be the first to propose
that the nominative issue lies at the center
of the question of the cannibal,
particularly the fictive (let's call it "mythic")

where the "eater" might also be understood
as, well, the murderer,
the rapist,
the Other,
what have you,
and where the "eaten"
is, you know, some exposition of the Self:
the Self in flux
the Self in crisis
the Self in California.

So we are curious about what happens
in that moment of identity
at which, presumably,
some periodicity of knowledge
is fully decoded and
inner causes become
outer effects.

If it is in your nature, somehow, that you are beyond the scope of
exegetical methodology
you should know that our first choice
is the phenomological purity of your violence
your own hot and wasteful grammar

replete with exclusionary principles, irrational desires
                rhetorics of meat and steam
                stylistics of twitch and spill
                economies of scale in which
pain is too well documented not to be instructive.

You see now how it is. You see what we need.

6

That is out and toward a deepening sense
of coiling
        or a gyre in the compass to seem
        universal in the touch, part of
        particular and is go, is without
deferrals of step beyond or
splendid ferns (if they are ferns) and back if they
come from the same seed and who will be
left
and writing in the woods is unwise
        is not on the conventional understanding
        a clear return to the trail (if it is a trail)
or make of these signs a turn
        from, a tear away,
        to take up the field
leave seasons to leaves and ineluctable grasses

who does not know what it is
to break the world where it is
weakest
        and finding a failure of memory
        to be (if it is home) your home

7

It is foundational that smash,
a machine of rock
requires the moving part
of your finger, holding up
the vertex of the pyramids,
from the inside, a hard place
to imagine in certain circles,
concentricities shifting on
divisible strengths to levers,
only knobs, only blood
under the vertex of your finger
held between teeth and ruin
for what is witnessed
what will hurt
and is the keeping sense
of archaeology
of what is archaic
of what will have been
bone

8

I am in the business just now of thinking
about the ontology of hidden objects

You can watch old films of Henry Moore
sculpting his world his impossible forms

of abstractions with secretly-human heads
trapped beneath the concurring rock

brutal harlequins burdened by monstrance
with idioms of standing and leaning and locking

I might invoke here the brick placed thus
in the manner of Daedalus, who after all

dreamed only of a bridge to Rhodes.

A Trivium for the Lost

I

I know a bookmaker in Atlanta
who claims to have a Wagnerian
tuba in his basement.

There was a time when I would struggle
with the implications of this kind of knowledge
            and wonder, for instance:
                what would it mean to understand this?
                What is the value of my trust?
And what, now that word is out, is my responsibility here?

II

He speaks in Noir-Punk,
is known to "land"
in "squalid joints"
on the "bitch-ass-edge" of town
and is forever "taking it on the lam" with
(or because of) some "brassy dame."

III

Of course, a story like this one
resists the usual modes of inquiry,
but it is worth observing that the principal
of contra-positive identity reveals a thing
through the catalogue of everything it is not.

Even the Greeks knew this.

Mountain Logic Above Tallulah Falls

Because the sky is not a transitivity
we are not known to

        subsume into the weight
        or the names of stones, wet

        and ripped from their formal properties,
        simple styles of confession.

And it is true enough that a certain craft
in geography

        inscribes the double integral
        of granite in the palm

        urgent as a lost memory, concomitant
        as fingers to the map.

Because I adduce from the foot to the Earth
I have been known to

        memorize the wrong words
        or hide glyphs inside my shoes

        and then wonder whether any of this
        constitutes a principled position.

My father found fragments of farming tools
buried in the backyard, lost to work and clay,

honest in the censure of summer's still heat.

There, too, he turned up slabs of mica
in transgressive excavations
of what was, after all, our own history
diffracted around these subterranean sacraments
of plunging and grinding
toward the empirical core of
what was, after all, our own mythology.

But I never saw him happier
than when a recalcitrant rock
pulled downward from his leverage
refusing to yield to Christian hands.

Because whomever is given or indeed whatever
is finally proved in the transitivity of

        waters moved distributively down
        to the reservoirs, to the ocean

        must yield to my waking
        pushing ever inscrutably,
        invisibly up

[65]

www.ingramcontent.com/pod-product-compliance
Lightning Source LLC
LaVergne TN
LVHW022318080426
835509LV00036B/2859